SKATEBOARDING

Raintree www.raintreepublishers.co.uk

To order:
Phone 44 (0) 1865 888112
Send a fax to 44 (0) 1865 314091
Visit the Raintree bookshop at
www.raintreepublishers.co.uk
to browse our catalogue and order online.

Produced by
David West 🏃 **Children's Books**
7 Princeton Court
55 Felsham Road
London SW15 1AZ

Picture Research: Carlotta Cooper
Designer: Gary Jeffrey
Editor: James Pickering

First published in Great Britain by
Raintree, Halley Court, Jordan Hill,
Oxford OX2 8EJ, part of Harcourt Education.
Raintree is a registered trademark of Harcourt
Education Ltd.

© David West Children's Books 2003
The moral right of the proprietor has been asserted.

Printed and bound in Italy

ISBN 1 844 43091 X (hardback)
07 06 05 04 03
10 9 8 7 6 5 4 3 2 1

ISBN 1 844 43096 0 (paperback)
08 07 06 05 04
10 9 8 7 6 5 4 3 2 1

British Library Cataloguing in Publication Data
Powell, Ben
Skateboarding. – (Extreme sports)
796.2'2
A full catalogue record for this book is available
from the British Library.

Acknowledgements
The publishers would like to thank the following
for permission to reproduce photographs:

Abbreviations: t-top, m-middle, b-bottom, r-right,
l-left, c-centre.

Front cover - Corbis Images. Pages 4-5, 6l & br, 7t,
8tr, 9l, 10-11, 18bl, 20tr - Will Linford. 5br, 8l,
11mr, 12-13t, 15tr, 16t, 21t, 22-23, 24 both, 26-
27b, 28l - Buzz Pictures. 6tr, 14tl, 16b - Corbis
Images. 7b, 25t - The Kobal Collection/AGI Orsi
Productions/Vans off the Wall/Darrin, Pat. 8br, 9r,
19br, 20tl & bl, 21b, 22l, 26l, 29 both - Leo
Sharpe. 10bl - Rex Features Ltd. 11bl & br, 13t -
Ben Powell. 25r - Lynn Cooper Productions LLC.
24-25b, 28tr - Andy Horsely. 26-27t - Steve
Glidewell.

*An explanation of difficult words can be
found in the glossary on page 31.*

extreme sports

SKATEBOARDING

Ben Powell

Raintree

CONTENTS

Introduction

Skateboarding was invented about 50 years ago, by surfers who wanted to practise their sport on land when they couldn't get out to sea. Only a few people used skateboards and, unlike today, the boards themselves were usually cheap and badly put together. Today, skateboarding is a huge global industry, and open to all. Experts and beginners equally can have lots of fun. Some people are happy cruising around the streets. Others choose to take risks on huge vert ramps, stairs or handrails. Just step on the board, push and join in the fun.

JUST GOOD FUN
Skateboarding has no rules or limits – no teams, no records to beat, just plain and simple fun.

STAY SAFE
It's always a good idea to wear a helmet when you're out skateboarding.

WARNING! SKATEBOARDING CAN BE AN **EXTREMELY DANGEROUS** SPORT. DO NOT ATTEMPT ANY MOVES **BEYOND YOUR ABILITIES** AND ALWAYS WEAR THE APPROPRIATE SAFETY EQUIPMENT.

The early years

The earliest skateboards were based on home-made wooden go-karts, or 'boxcars'. Take away the handle of the boxcar, and you were left with a simple skateboard.

The craze begins

In the late 1950s, American and European toy makers picked up on the home-made skateboard craze, and started to sell the first factory-made skateboards. Shaped like a surfboard, these boards seem very old fashioned today – their clay wheels disintegrated after just a few hours. It was only in the 1960s that skateboarding began to take off. The sport became accepted as part of the Californian surf scene, and for the first time, skateboards were seen as more than just children's toys.

KICKTURN
An early skater kickturns (raises the front wheels) in a concrete park.

DESIGN
Early skateboards were shaped like surfboards with a nose and tail.

FULLPIPE
Skaters were soon exploring all sorts of obstacles. A fullpipe (left) is a circular wall – to get round it, you need to skate upside down!

POLYURETHANE

Polyurethane plastic wheels were invented in 1973. These allowed skaters to ride on almost any surface.

Boom

Skateboarding was huge between 1975 and 1978. The top skateboarders became superstars overnight. Huge concrete skateparks were built, and big business began to catch on. Skateboarding was used to advertise everything from soft drinks to toys, and all around the world millions of people caught the skateboarding bug.

POOL SKATING

Many of the basic tricks and techniques that still survive today were invented in empty pools like this. The hard concrete surface made them dangerous places.

Bust

Unfortunately, the 1970s skateboarding boom was short-lived. Injured skateboarders took legal action against the skateparks where they had been hurt. Some parks were badly designed in the first place and went out of business. Most of the large public skateparks were demolished and turned back into car parks. As a result, skateboard manufacturers also went out of business – with nowhere to ride, few people were interested in buying skateboards.

The backyard resistance

Skateboarding went right out of fashion in the early 1980s. Nevertheless, a dedicated band of skaters kept the sport alive. They knew they could no longer rely on custom-built skateparks which might be here today and gone tomorrow.

Fall out

The companies that had supported skateboarding in the 1970s wanted to make money fast – they were rarely interested in the long-term survival of the sport. Skateboarding had gone from obscurity to popularity and back to obscurity in just five years. Serious skaters were determined that the sport should survive. They started to customize and adapt their boards to suit themselves. Skaters are still doing this today.

FABIAN KRAVETZ
Fabian Kravetz was a well-known freestyle skater in the 1980s. He put a cartoon image of himself on his board.

KICKFLIP
Jamie Bolland was another star of 1980s skateboarding. Here, he demonstrates a kickflip (see page 18).

Take-over

Even during the 1980s, it was still possible to buy high-quality skateboard products, but now the people running the skate companies were actually skateboarders themselves. Professional skaters, such as Stacey Peralta and Tony Alva, went into business making boards for a small but thriving market of committed skateboarders.

MIKE McGILL
Mike McGill demonstrates an air for the crowd at a vertical demonstration in the late 1980s.

Back to the streets

Skaters wanted to find 'natural' alternatives to the obstacles in man-made skateparks. Empty outdoor swimming pools, banked playgrounds, rails and steps all proved popular. Riders made small wooden ramps and halfpipes (two gradually sloping walls) which copied skatepark obstacles at an affordable price. Skateboarding went back to its roots as a street sport, and moved away from the rules and regulations of the mid 1970s.

UP AND OVER
A rider flips over a handrail and on to a concrete wave in a city park. Doing this kind of extreme trick without safety gear is very dangerous.

BIG BOARD
Boards in the 1980s were much wider and heavier than they had been in the past.

Underground

Slowly but surely, interest in skateboarding began to grow again as skaters took control of the industry themselves. It was now a vital and permanent part of street culture. Skateboarding companies and advertisers tried to appeal to the 'underground' market, as the latest fashion and music became tied in with the sport. Skateboarding was no longer just a craze.

Evolution - street skating

Skateboarding had always been divided into rigid disciplines. There were three clear groups - bowl (ramp riding), freestyle (skating on a flat surface) and slalom (skating around obstacles).

Evolution

When skateboarding went out of fashion in the late 1970s, the rules that governed the sport also crumbled. The most important trick that was invented in this period was the flat ground ollie (see page 16). Alan Gelfand first invented the ollie or 'hands-free aerial' in a skatepark – but this trick also revolutionized street skating. Without the ollie, skateboarding would never have developed into the sport we know today.

OLLIE GRIND

Paul Silvester uses an ollie (see page 16) to launch himself into a grind down a skatepark ramp.

THE ULTIMATE BOARD

In all three *Back to the Future* films, Michael J. Fox played Marty McFly. In the second film, he rode a futuristic hoverboard to get out of trouble!

HOORAY FOR HOLLYWOOD

Skateboarding started to pick up again in the late 1980s, particularly street skating. Several successful films featured street skating, including the *Back to the Future* and *Police Academy* films, which sparked a real revival all around the world. More and more skaters started street skating – a hard surface and a skateboard were all that they needed.

TONY HAWK
Tony Hawk shows the crowd a backside air.

Hawk and the X-Games

In the late 1990s, a new competition emerged. The X-Games introduced skateboarding, BMX, inline skating and other extreme sports to a global audience of millions. Tony Hawk became a TV star and the biggest name in skateboarding. He endorsed a fantastically successful skateboard computer game, which encouraged a whole new generation to take up the sport.

GUIDE #1

RISE OF THE SKATE VIDEO

Stacey Peralta was one of the first people to make his living from skateboarding in the 1970s. He also produced the early *Bones Brigade* skate videos which featured a young Tony Hawk. If you want to see skateboarding at its best, performed by the experts, look out for Blind skateboard's *Video Days* from 1991 and Plan B's *Questionable* (1992). The skateboarding in these films still looks incredible today, over ten years after their original release.

Most magazines and board companies produce videos.

The four main parts of a skateboard have hardly changed over the last 20 years. The deck, trucks, bearings and wheels have remained the same, simply because they cannot be improved upon.

The deck

The part of the skateboard that you stand on – the deck – is made of laminated Canadian maple wood. This particular wood is used because it's springy and flexible. As skateboarding became more technical and reliant on tricks, riders wanted smaller decks that were easy to control. Most of the large and unusual board designs of the early 1980s had disappeared by the early 1990s. The straight 'lollipop' shaped deck became the standard skateboard design. It was much better suited to the demands of modern skateboarding than the earlier 'fish-tailed' boards.

☻ DESIGNER BOARD

Different board companies have their own unique designs that they put on their decks.

The trucks

The truck is the wheel mechanism, and a vital part of the board. Trucks have become lighter and smaller over the years. The hanger holds the axle that your wheels attach to. It's also the surface you grind along. Rubbers, or grommets, sit on either side of the hanger and allow the truck to turn. The kingpin is a bolt that runs through the hanger and rubbers and sits in the baseplate on a plastic pivot cup. The baseplate is bolted to the deck and holds the truck together.

Axle

Kingpin

Rubbers

Hanger

Baseplate

TUFF LOVE SERIES Death

Deck

GRAPHICS
Individual graphics – like this skull, crossbones and barcode design – don't just look good. They make your board much easier to recover if it's been lost or stolen.

Griptape
This is a self-adhesive sandpaper-like material that sits on your deck and allows your feet to grip the board.

Truck

Wheels
Frank Nasworthy was the Californian inventor who devised polyurethane plastic wheels about 30 years ago. These have been fitted to practically every skateboard ever since. You can buy wheels of different sizes and weights. Most skaters today choose wheels no smaller than 50 millimetres. The durometer reading is a measurement of how hard the polyurethane is. Harder wheels are most suitable for rugged terrain. Most wheels have a durometer reading of between 95 and 100.

Bearings

Hex nut

Polyurethane wheel

SKATEBOARDING 13

Basic techniques

Before they even think about moving on to basic tricks, all new skaters should first learn the basics of standing, pushing and turning.

Goofy stance skaters stand with their right foot forward.

Regular skaters stand with the left foot at the front of the board.

Stances

There are two stances in skateboarding – 'regular' and 'goofy'. Everyone has a stance that feels more natural to them, just like being right- or left-handed. The best way to find out which stance you prefer is simply to stand on a board. See what feels more comfortable – regular or goofy.

SMOOTH RIDE
Always keep your knees bent on the board.

Pushing

Place your front foot on the board with your toe pointing towards the nose. Leave your back foot on the floor and push yourself along gently. As your back foot pushes off, transfer your weight on to your front foot. As you start to move, turn your front foot so that it is horizontal across your board, and put your back foot on to the tail of your board.

PUSHING OFF
Start on a smooth, level surface to begin with and practise pushing until you feel confident. As with everything else in skateboarding, learning to push takes time.

GUIDE #2

HOW TO DO A KICKTURN

Quarterpipe transition

Kickturns

Find a gentle slope or a quarterpipe at a local skatepark. Push gently towards the incline (transition). As you reach the peak of the slope, turn your shoulders, lift up your front wheels and turn through 180 degrees, so that you are facing in the opposite direction. Ride away.

QUARTERPIPE

A quarterpipe is a small, gently sloping ramp.

Frontside and backside

Frontside and backside refer to the direction in which you do your kickturn (or any other trick). If you kickturn with your back facing the platform of a quarterpipe, you're in a backside kickturn. If you turn with your chest facing the platform then you're turning in a frontside direction. Like many tricks and techniques in skateboarding, these terms are taken from surfing.

The ollie

The ollie is the most important trick you can learn. Virtually every stunt in skateboarding has an ollie in there somewhere. It's a difficult trick to pick up and takes a lot of practice to master.

The ollie - technique

When you're starting out, it's best to practise the ollie on a soft surface such as a carpet or a lawn, to cut down the risks of bumps and bruises!

3 Crouch and pop your tail off the floor with your back foot. Lift yourself upwards and angle your front foot so that it slides up the board.

1 Stand on your board with your back foot on the tail, with your toes right at the very edge. Put your front foot horizontally across the middle of your board. Transfer your weight to and from the tail.

2 Get your timing right. You need to hit your tail against the floor with your back foot, and immediately jump upwards whilst controlling your board with your front foot.

4 As you scrape your front foot up the board, lift your back foot up too, so that your board levels out.

The ollie - history

The ollie was invented by a skater called Alan Gelfand in the early 1980s. Alan lived and skated in Florida, USA. His nickname was Ollie – that's how this no-handed aerial trick got its name.

ON THE UP

The professional skater Blayney Hamilton ollies up some steps in Ireland, in 2002.

Please remember – the ollie is a very difficult trick to learn, but without it you won't be able to tackle other tricks. If you concentrate on mastering a clean and smooth ollie, you'll be able to progress on to more complicated and impressive moves.

5 Try to stay level in the air. That way, you'll land on all four wheels at once and with your weight balanced.

6 Land cleanly, crouching down to absorb the impact. Gradually stand back upright and ride away.

LONGBOARD

An ollie is combined with a nose grab (clutching the front end) on a longboard.

GUIDE #3

GRABS

ALL TUCKED UP

This is known as a tuck-knee, a variation of the basic indy grab (see below).

Ollies can be hands-free or you can grab your board at the peak of the ollie. There are various types of grabs, and their names usually refer to the part of the board you're grabbing. These are some of the most common grabs.

Indy – Grabbing the toe side of the board with your back hand over your back knee.

Mute – Grabbing the toe side of the board with your front hand over your front knee.

Melanchollie (or backside grab) – Grabbing the heel side of your board with your front hand.

Stalefish – Grabbing the heel side of your board with your back hand.

Tailgrab – Grabbing the tail of your board with your back hand.

Intermediate tricks

Once you've mastered the ollie and feel comfortable on your board, there are thousands of tricks to learn. The following tricks are fairly basic, but they can be tweaked, or varied, in all sorts of different ways. In skateboarding, as in every sport, it's important to learn the basics before you start pulling stunts.

1 & 2 Approach the ledge at a slight angle. Go at a speed you feel comfortable with, but no faster.

3 Do an ollie high enough to get above the ledge. Aim to land your trucks on the grinding edge.

4 As your hangers land on the ledge, lean back to absorb the impact. Make sure you don't fly off your board forwards.

50-50 grinds

This trick was created in skateparks. You need to force your truck's hangers against a hard surface and grind along it for a moment. On the street, beginners should start by tackling the 50-50 on the kerb, or any low surface.

GUIDE #4

KICKFLIPS

Keep your back foot on the edge of the tail, as you would for a normal ollie. Your front foot should be just behind your front truck bolts, and at a slight angle, so you can flip the edge of the board. Don't be tempted to put your front foot further back, towards your back truck bolts. The kickflip will rotate too near the ground and won't look so good.

Almost an ollie
The kickflip is a variation of the ollie, and the technique is quite similar.

Boardslides
The boardslide is another trick that was first created in the skatepark. You slide along an edge on the underside (belly) of your deck. The speed and length of your slide depends on what obstacle you choose to slide down.

6 As you slow down at the end of your grind, do a gentle ollie and get off the ledge.

7 As always, land with four wheels down.

5 As you lean back, feel the grinding motion, and try to stay relaxed but in control. Shuffle your feet back for a gentle ollie, and grind if you need to.

🕱 NOSEGRIND

The nosegrind is a variation of the 50-50, where you grind the front truck on an obstacle.

8 Crouch to absorb the impact. Ride away.

1 Approach the bar with your feet in the ollie position. **2** Do an ollie and get above the bar. **3** Turn round 90 degrees. **4** Land on the middle of your board. **5** Turn your shoulders and come off the end of the bar pointing forwards. **6** Land with all four wheels down at once. Ride away.

🕱 HANDRAIL GRIND

A skateboarder adapts the boardslide for the street. This is a frontside boardslide on a real handrail.

Advanced skating

Professional skateboarders base their styles on the three basic techniques: bowl, freestyle and slalom. Even the pros wobbled when they first stepped on a board.

Progression

The main difference between simple and advanced skating is the choice of obstacles. Beginners tend to stick to grinding down a kerb or riding a small skatepark quarterpipe. But a professional will look for the biggest, scariest and most awkward obstacles. Skateboarders are always trying to progress and push the sport to new extremes. Once you learn the basic tricks, you can take your skills into new and exciting terrain.

RAIL GRIND
Canadian professional skateboarder Rick McCrank nosegrinds down a handrail in London.

DOUG
A professional skater, known only as Doug, grasps a frontside air in a concrete park in Oregon, USA.

Riding switch

One of the most skilful, but often unseen, professional tricks is switch-stance or 'switch' skating. This means riding and performing tricks in the stance that feels least natural to you – goofy if you're naturally regular, and regular if you're goofy. Skating switch feels strange at first, just like writing with the 'wrong' hand. But your technique will change and improve, and if you practise, you'll be able to do twice as many tricks!

360 FLIP
Vaughan Baker skates for the Blueprint company. Here, he performs a 360 flip down a set of stairs.

Vert skating

Vertical, or ramp, skating has
progressed as quickly as street skating.
Just two decades ago, a ramp jump
was a simple grabbed 180 trick. These
days vert skaters regularly kickflip into spins of
360 and 540 degrees. Airs can be over
4 metres high. Millions of viewers around the world
have watched skaters at the X-Games tackle spins
of 720 and even 900 degrees.

STALEFISH GRAB

Among young skaters, vertical skating isn't as
popular as it was, but it's still the most difficult and
respected form of skateboarding. This is a huge
frontside stalefish grab at London's Urban Games.

GUIDE #5

'HAMMERS'

Stunt skaters, or 'hammer men', perform basic tricks on the
longest, highest and scariest obstacles they can find. The
hammers are so popular that huge handrails, flights of
steps and all sorts of dangerous skate obstacles have been
a regular feature of skateboard magazines and videos for
the last five years or so.

LOOK BEFORE YOU LEAP

Skating at this advanced level can be very dangerous.
Only experienced skaters have enough control and
skill to escape serious injury if
something goes wrong.

Safety gear and protection

Apart from vert skaters (who tackle vertical ramps), most professional skaters don't wear safety equipment. But beginners should always wear the four main pieces of safety gear.

Buckle up

The four main pieces of safety gear have been carefully designed to protect the parts of your body that are most likely to be injured if you fall off your board. How much gear you wear depends on the sort of riding you're doing. Use your common sense. You won't need full padding if you're riding a flat surface – it makes it difficult to move, and you won't pick up tricks so quickly. But wrist guards and knee pads are essential, because you definitely will fall off from time to time!

Elbow pads

Your elbows can be badly injured if you're skating big ramps or concrete transitions. Like knee pads, these are made from neoprene plastic. You fasten them around your arms with velcro straps.

☠ STAYING SAFE

For vert riding, full safety equipment is essential if you want to avoid serious injury.

Knee pads

These are the most commonly used pieces of safety gear. A plastic cup fits over your kneecap. This lets you slide out of falls, rather than landing with a thud and taking all the impact on your knees.

CUSTOMIZE IT
You can brighten up a dull-looking helmet with stickers and graphics.

Some skateparks require pads, some do not. Always check before you skate.

Helmets
You'll need a helmet if you're learning to skate on a vert ramp or in a big concrete park. You should make sure that the helmet fits correctly and has a foam lining and tight chin strap to hold it on securely. A specialist skateboard shop will find the right helmet for you.

Wrist guards
Wrist guards stop you from twisting your wrists. Skateboarders often break their wrists – you should wear wrist guards until you're confident enough to fall without hurting yourself.

COMMON SKATEBOARDING INJURIES
Apart from cuts and bruises, the 'tweaked ankle' is the most common skateboarding injury. It is usually caused by landing with all your weight on the side of your foot, causing your ankle to swell up rapidly and throb with pain.

Remember the golden rule – R.I.C.E.
Rest – give your body time to recover before you start skating again.
Ice – an ice pack will reduce pain and swelling.
Compression – bandage your ankle tightly.
Elevation – put your foot up. This will also reduce swelling.

Legends of skateboarding

Like any other sport, skateboarding has its fair share of legends and heroes. These riders use their skill and imagination to push out the boundaries, and influence millions of skaters around the world.

Tony Hawk

Tony is the most famous skater of all time. He invented many of vert skating's most difficult tricks. He has kept his position at the very top of the professional vert skateboarding scene for more than 15 years. Tony is also a successful businessman – he runs the skate company Birdhouse, the shoe company Adio, a chain of shops and he promotes a number of computer games.

TONY HAWK

With his knees pressed against his shoulders, Tony Hawk demonstrates a superb indy at a public display.

JOHN RATTRAY

John has a busy travel and filming schedule. Here, he grinds down a park rail in Belfast, Northern Ireland.

John Rattray

Born and raised in Aberdeen, Scotland, John's raw talent, fluid style and dedication have taken him far from home. Originally John rode for the UK company Blueprint, but he's now riding for the US company Zero.

Tony Alva

Tony Alva is the grandfather of modern skateboarding. He invented the first airborne trick – the frontside air. Tony grew up in a suburb of Los Angeles, USA and found fame in the 1970s with his aggressive style. Tony stuck with the sport after the 1970s crash and was one of the first people to try skating in an empty outdoor swimming pool.

👤 TONY ALVA

Tony Alva featured in the film *Dogtown and Z-Boys*, which charted the early history of skateboarding.

Duane Peters

Another Californian legend, Duane invented many tricks, and was the first person to do a loop-the-loop around a fullpipe – skating upside down! Duane is perhaps best known for his rebellious style and colourful outfits. He's also a musician, and even in his forties, he still performs with his successful punk band the US Bombs.

👤 DUANE PETERS

Duane invented this invert trick. These clothes were the height of fashion in the 1980s.

Tom Penny

Tom is the most famous UK skateboarder. He moved to the USA in 1995, where he and fellow skateboarder, Geoff Rowley, invented a new relaxed style. Tom disappeared from the professional circuit at the height of his fame, turning himself into a legend overnight.

👤 TOM PENNY

Tom recently reappeared in the skateboard video *Sorry*.

There are two main types of terrain where you can skate - street and skatepark. But there are thousands of different obstacles and challenges in each of these places. Use your imagination to push yourself to new extremes.

Skatepark
Wooden skateparks exist all over the world. This skatepark offers driveways, spines, boxes and launches (ramps you can launch yourself from).

Street

'Street' terrain can mean anything from the flat ground of a car park to the steps, handrails and blocks found in any city. Once you've mastered the basics on your board, you can turn a useless area into a place to have serious fun! But it's worth remembering that in certain places street skating is not allowed. There may even be local laws that prohibit skateboarding in particular areas. Make sure you're aware of your surroundings and show consideration for those who live near by. Litter or graffiti will almost certainly lead to your spot being shut down.

🖐 **URBAN FLYER!**
John Fisher ollies down a big set of steps in Derby, England.

Wooden skateparks

Most skateparks have a variety of curved ramps and halfpipes of different sizes. You can ride on mini ramps — scaled-down versions of vert ramps where you can learn the basic tricks. On a spine ramp, two ramps join together without a platform in between them. Vert ramps are the largest ramps of all, with transitions that reach vertical. There are also banks, blocks and bars to ride.

Concrete skateparks

Riding in a concrete skatepark feels very different from riding in a wooden park. Concrete is a much harder material than wood so you can ride much faster and get more grip, but it's more painful to fall on. Some concrete parks have the same sort of man-made ramps you find in a wooden park, only bigger — bowls, banks and halfpipes. Others recreate the rails and other obstacles you might see in a city street. Modern skateboarding was born in concrete parks in the 1970s. All riders should try skating in a concrete park, but don't forget that skateparks can be dangerous places for beginners.

WOOD IS GOOD

Most contests and events are held on wooden, mobile ramps like these.

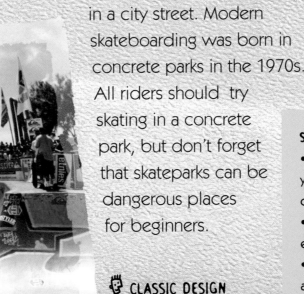

CLASSIC DESIGN

Marseilles skatepark in France is world famous for the smoothness of its surface and the perfection of its design.

SKATEPARK ETHICS

- Don't go to skateparks until you've mastered the basics of skateboarding.
- Stay out of the way of more experienced skaters.
- Try to stick to the beginners' area until you are confident.
- Never sit on obstacles — other skaters will collide with you.
- Keep well back and follow the lines on the ground to work out where to cross and where to skate yourself.

The global skateboard scene

Skateboarding is a huge global sport, and these days skateparks can be found in most large towns and cities. They're the best places to get professional advice and help.

The worldwide scene

Skateboarding events and competitions take place every week of the year, and you should be able to find one close to where you live. You could even get together with friends and start your own event. That's the beauty of skateboarding – there are no rules whatsoever. Skate festivals, where major competitions take place, are great places to meet other skaters and exchange ideas. But there are also plenty of less serious events where you can pick up new tricks.

AUSTRALIA

A vert skater drifts backside above a huge wooden vert ramp in Australia. At contests, you can see skating on all types of terrain.

UK SCENE

Professional skater Kareem Campbell in mid-flip above a ramp in Radlands, Northampton, UK.

Tampa

Dortmund

Marseilles

Livingston

LIVI

Livingston in Scotland is host to the 'Pure Fun Skate Party' every June and July at the huge concrete skatepark known affectionately as 'Livi'.

Festivals and competitions

One of the best known US competitions takes place in Tampa, Florida. It features professional and amateur skaters, and has been running for over ten years. Unlike other festivals, the Tampa event isn't run by big businesses, but by skaters themselves, who are passionate about their sport. Dortmund in Germany hosts a massive European skate competition in July every year. These 'Monster Masterships' attract skaters from all over the world.

MARSEILLES

Marseilles in the South of France is home to one of Europe's best-loved concrete parks. This beach front park attracts thousands of visitors every year, especially to the Bowl Riders' Cup in early June. Go to www.skateboardeurope.com for details and dates.

Useful information

Skateboard magazines, websites and videos provide information on everything from competitions to new skate spots. These are just a few of the many available.

MAGAZINES & PERIODICALS

Sidewalk

British skateboard magazine with firm roots in the UK scene. Also featuring European and US skating.

Sugar

High quality French skateboard magazine with features from all over Europe.

Transworld Skateboarding

Glossy US magazine with plenty of photos of the top professionals.

Thrasher magazine

Another US magazine, emphasizing the skate culture, fashions and the various styles of skating.

Skateboarder magazine

Well written US skateboard magazine – the thinking skater's choice.

INTERNATIONAL EVENTS

Europe:

Dortmund, Germany 'Monsterships'.

Go to www.skateboardeurope.com.

Lausanne, Switzerland, bi-annual World Championships.

Go to www.skateboardeurope.com.

Marseilles, France, Bowlriders' Cup.

Go to www.skateboardeurope.com.

Livingston, Scotland, Pure Fun Skate Party.

Go to www.sidewalkmag.com for UK events listings.

USA:

Tampa Pro/Am series.

Go to www.skateparkoftampa.com for details.

WEBSITES

www.skateboardeurope.com

www.skateboarding.com

www.thrashermagazine.com

www.pendrekmagazine.com

www.sidewalkmag.com

www.skateboardermag.com

All the Internet addresses (URLs) given in this book were valid at the time of going to press. However, due to the dynamic nature of the Internet, some addresses may have changed, or sites may have ceased to exist since publication. While the author and publishers regret any inconvenience this may cause readers, no responsibility for any such changes can be accepted by either the author or the publishers.

Glossary

air

any move that involves leaving the ground on your skateboard. You can grab your board during an air, you can ollie into it, or you can perform airs in pools, skateparks or from ramps.

bearings

small metal rings that sit inside your wheels, allowing them to turn

bowl

skateboard obstacle that copies the oval shape of an outdoor swimming pool. Bowls come in many different shapes and sizes, and are usually built from concrete.

customize

alter the appearance of your board by adding extras, such as different wheels, bearings, trucks, stickers, spray paint and novelty griptape

ethics

unwritten code of conduct in skateboarding, such as looking after skate spots, skating sensibly and being friendly and uncompetitive

flatground

skateboarding tricks that involve balancing and flipping on a flat surface

fliptrick

any trick involving a rotation or 'flip' of the board. There are countless variations, named after the type of flipping motion or the technique used.

freestyle

early discipline of skateboarding based on tricks and jumps on flat ground

grind

force your trucks along a hard edge

halfpipe

ramp with two curved (transitioned) walls. Many different variations and sizes exist, but any U-shaped ramp is called a halfpipe.

polyurethane

plastic material used to make skateboard wheels. Before polyurethane wheels were invented, skaters had to make do with clay wheels that were very fragile and couldn't be used on uneven surfaces.

professional (pro)

skater who earns a living by skateboarding. Most professionals put their names to (endorse) their own boards, as well as signature model shoes, wheels and clothing.

switch stance

riding your skateboard in both the regular and goofy styles

transition

curved arc of a ramp, where tricks are done

vert ramp

curved ramp with a transition that reaches a vertical angle